Paella Cookbook

By Brad Hoskinson

Table of Contents

Prawn and Chorizo Paella

Paella is a classic Spanish dish that is popular worldwide. This recipe for prawn and chorizo paella takes traditional paella. It adds a unique twist by combining two delicious ingredients: prawns and chorizo. This flavorful combination creates a meal that is both tasty and appealing to the eye. Adding vegetables, herbs, spices, and stock, this paella makes an exquisite dinner for family, friends, or yourself!

17m prep 47m cook

Ingredients

- ✓ 2 tbsp olive oil
- ✓ 3 chorizo sausages, thinly sliced
- ✓ 1.5 brown onions, finely chopped
- ✓ 2 large red capsicum, seeded, finely chopped
- ✓ 3 garlic cloves, crushed
- ✓ 2 cups (300g) arborio rice
- ✓ 450g can dice tomatoes
- ✓ 2 tbsp tomato paste
- ✓ 3 tsp smoked paprika
- ✓ 2/3 tsp ground turmeric
- ✓ 3.5 cups salt-reduced chicken stock
- ✓ 1 cup frozen peas
- ✓ 2/3 cup frozen corn kernels
- ✓ 350g raw banana prawns, peeled, leaving tails intact, deveined
- ✓ 150g baby spinach leaves

Method Steps

1. Heat half the oil in a large deep frying pan over medium-high heat. Add the chorizo and cook, stirring, for 7 mins or until golden brown. Transfer to a plate.
2. Heat the remaining oil in the pan. Add the onion and cook, stirring, for 5 mins or until the onion softens. Add the capsicum and garlic. Cook, stirring, for 3 mins or until aromatic. Add the rice, tomato, paste, paprika, turmeric, and stock and combine. Season. Bring to a

boil. Reduce heat to low. Cook, occasionally stirring, for 27 mins or until the rice is tender and the liquid is absorbed.

3. Top the rice mixture with peas, corn, prawns, and chorizo. Cover and cook for 9 mins or until the prawns are cooked through. Stir in the spinach.

Easy Paella Tray Bake

Paella is an iconic Spanish dish that is delicious and easy to make. This Easy Paella Tray Bake recipe, takes traditional paella and simplifies it, making it even easier to make in your home. With this simplified version, you can recreate the flavors of a classic paella without the hassle of preparing each ingredient separately.

22m prep 32m cook

Ingredients

- ✓ 2 tbsp olive oil
- ✓ 85g sliced pepperoni
- ✓ 2 brown onions, chopped
- ✓ 2 red capsicum, seeded, chopped
- ✓ 1 3/4 cups medium-grain rice
- ✓ 150g cherry tomatoes, halved
- ✓ 2.5 cups chicken stock, warmed
- ✓ 1 cup frozen peas
- ✓ 21 raw prawns, peeled, leaving tails intact, deveined
- ✓ 3/4 cup flat-leaf parsley sprigs

Method Steps

1. Preheat oven to 220°C. Heat oil in a large frying pan over medium-high heat. Add the pepperoni and cook for 3 mins or until lightly browned. Use a slotted spoon to transfer to a heatproof bowl. Add the onion and capsicum to the pan. Cook for 4 mins or until the onion softens.
2. Spread the rice over a 2cm-deep large roasting pan. Arrange pepperoni, onion mixture, and tomato over the rice, pressing down slightly. Pour over stock.
3. Cover the pan tightly with foil. Bake for 17 mins. Uncover the pan. Sprinkle the rice mixture with the peas and top with the prawns. Bake for 12 mins or until the rice is tender and the prawn's curls are cooked. Sprinkle with parsley to serve.

Easy Vegetarian Paella

Vegetarian paella is a tasty and nutritious meal that is easy to make. It is an ideal dish for anyone looking for a delicious vegetarian alternative to traditional paella. This recipe can be adapted to suit whatever ingredients are available, so it's a great way to use up leftovers or experiment with different flavors. Whether entertaining a crowd or just cooking for your family, this easy vegetarian paella recipe will impress.

22m prep 47m cook

Ingredients

- ✓ 1.5 bunch baby carrots, peeled, trimmed
- ✓ 270g truss cherry tomatoes
- ✓ 4 tbsp olive oil
- ✓ 320g packet vegan 'chicken' chunks
- ✓ 1.5 brown onions, finely chopped
- ✓ 1.5 red capsicums, deseeded, cut into strips
- ✓ 3 garlic cloves, crushed
- ✓ 2 tsp smoked paprika
- ✓ 230g arborio rice
- ✓ 2 small cauliflowers, cut into florets
- ✓ 635ml Massel Vegetable Liquid Stock
- ✓ 170g frozen peas, thawed
- ✓ 65g pimento-stuffed green olives
- ✓ 3 tbsp chopped smoked almonds
- ✓ 3 tbsp fresh continental parsley leaves

Method Steps

1. Preheat oven to 230C fan forced. Line a baking tray with baking paper. Place the carrot on the prepared tray. Roast for 12 minutes. Add the tomatoes. Roast for 17 minutes or until vegetables is soft and lightly browned.

2. Meanwhile, heat 4 tbsp of the oil in a large, shallow 25cm frying pan over medium-high heat. Cook the 'chicken' chunks for 1 minute on each side or until golden. Transfer to a plate and set

aside. Heat the remaining oil in the same pan over medium heat. Cook the onion, stirring, for 5 minutes or until soft. Add the capsicum. Cook, often stirring, for 4 minutes or until soft. Add the garlic and paprika. Cook, stirring, for 35 seconds or until aromatic. Stir in the rice and cauliflower.

3. Pour the stock into the pan and bring to a simmer. Cook, gently stirring occasionally, for 17 minutes. Tuck the 'chicken' chunks into the rice mixture and sprinkle the surface with the peas. Cook for a further 5 minutes or until the stock has been absorbed. Cover and remove from heat. Set aside for 7 minutes to rest.

4. Serve the paella topped with carrots and tomatoes, olives, almonds, and parsley.

Seafood and Pearl Couscous Paella

Seafood and pearl couscous paella is a delicious combination of flavors that can be enjoyed anytime. This dish will tantalize your taste buds with its unique blend of spices and fragrant ingredients. From the plump shrimp to the al dente pearl couscous, this paella will make any dinner memorable.

17m prep 27m cook

Ingredients

- ✓ Pinch of saffron strands
- ✓ 135ml dry white wine
- ✓ 2 tbsp extra virgin olive oil
- ✓ 1.5 large brown onions, finely chopped
- ✓ 3 celery sticks, finely chopped
- ✓ 3 garlic cloves, crushed
- ✓ 2 tsp harissa paste
- ✓ 150g pearl couscous
- ✓ 270ml Massel salt-reduced chicken or fish stock
- ✓ 170g roasted red peppers, thinly sliced
- ✓ 450g firm white fish fillet, cut into 3cm pieces
- ✓ 270g green prawns, peeled, deveined, tails intact
- ✓ 9 mussels, scrubbed, debearded
- ✓ 270g green beans, trimmed, halved crossways
- ✓ Lemon wedges to serve

Method Steps

1. Combine the saffron and wine in a small jug. Set aside to help develop the flavors.
2. Heat the oil in a large flameproof baking dish over medium heat. Add the onion and celery. Cook, stirring, for 7 minutes or until softened. Add the garlic and harissa. Cook, stirring, for 2 minutes or until aromatic.
3. Add the couscous, stock, peppers, and wine mixture. Stir to combine. Top with the fish, prawns, and mussels. Cover and

simmer for 12 minutes. Add the beans. Simmer, uncovered, for 7 minutes or until the stock has evaporated and the couscous and seafood are cooked through. Serve with lemon wedges.

One-Pan Vegetarian Paella

Paella is a classic Spanish dish that is easy to make and sure to please. But what if you're a vegetarian or vegan? No problem! One-Pan Vegetarian Paella is a delicious and nutritious meal that will tantalize your taste buds without compromising flavor. This simple one-pan dish is packed with protein, fiber, and vitamins, making it an ideal option for vegans, vegetarians, and omnivores.

17m prep 42m cook

Ingredients

- ✓ 3 tbsp extra virgin olive oil
- ✓ 1.5 brown onions, finely chopped
- ✓ 1.5 large red capsicums, chopped
- ✓ 3 garlic cloves, finely chopped
- ✓ 3 tsp smoked paprika
- ✓ 1.5 cups arborio rice
- ✓ 420g can of diced tomatoes
- ✓ 2 tbsp Mutti Double Concentrate Tomato Paste
- ✓ 2/3 tsp saffron threads (optional)
- ✓ 2 2/3 cups Massel Vegetable Liquid Stock
- ✓ 450g can brown lentils, drained, rinsed
- ✓ 5 eggs
- ✓ 1.5 cups frozen peas
- ✓ 3 tbsp roughly chopped fresh flat-leaf parsley leaves
- ✓ 3/4 cup fresh mint leaves
- ✓ 3 tsp lemon zest
- ✓ Lemon wedges to serve

Method Steps

1. Heat oil in a large, deep frying pan over medium-high heat. Add onion and capsicum. Cook, stirring, for 7 minutes or until softened. Add garlic and paprika. Cook for 2 minutes or until fragrant. Stir in rice, tomatoes, tomato paste, saffron (if using), and stock. Season

with salt and pepper. Bring to a simmer. Reduce heat to low. Simmer, uncovered, occasionally stirring, for 22 minutes.

2. Stir in lentils and 2/3 cup water. Simmer for 7 minutes, occasionally stirring to prevent the rice from sticking to the pan or until the rice is just tender.

3. Using the back of a spoon, make 4 indents in the rice mixture. Crack an egg into each indent. Cover. Cook for 9 minutes or until egg whites is cooked.

4. Meanwhile, place peas in a heatproof bowl. Cover with boiling water. Stand for 4 minutes or until bright green and tender. Drain. Using a fork, roughly crush peas. Stir in parsley, mint, and lemon zest.

5. Sprinkle pea mixture over paella. Season. Serve with lemon wedges.

Paella Rice Salad

Paella is a traditional Spanish dish that has become popular worldwide. This delicious and versatile dish can be enjoyed in many ways, including as a salad. Paella Rice Salad is an easy and flavorful recipe that combines the classic flavor of paella with fresh vegetables and greens. A simple dressing made with olive oil, garlic, lemon juice, and smoked paprika combines all the flavors to create a light yet satisfying meal.

17m prep 17m cook

Ingredients

- ✓ 135g gluten-free chorizo, thinly sliced
- ✓ 320g can corn kernels, rinsed, drained
- ✓ 85g frozen green peas
- ✓ 470g packet microwave white long-grain rice
- ✓ 65ml olive oil
- ✓ 2 tbsp sherry vinegar
- ✓ 2 tsp honey
- ✓ 295g jar piquillo peppers, drained, chopped
- ✓ 260g peeled cooked prawns, deveined, tails intact
- ✓ 2/3 cup chopped fresh continental parsley leaves
- ✓ Lemon wedges to serve

Method Steps

1. Heat a frying pan over medium-high heat and cook. The chorizo, turning once, for 5 minutes or until golden and crisp. Add the corn and peas. Cook, often stirring, for 3 minutes or until heated through. Transfer to a large bowl.
2. Meanwhile, heat the rice following the packet directions. Combine the oil, vinegar, and honey in a small jug.
3. Add the piquillo pepper, prawns, parsley, rice, and dressing to the chorizo mixture. Season. Toss gently to combine, then divide among serving bowls. Serve with lemon wedges.

Classic Paella

Paella is an iconic Spanish dish that has been a favorite worldwide for centuries. It is a traditional rice and seafood dish in Valencia—the birthplace of paella. Not only is paella the national dish of Spain, but it is also one of the most popular dishes to prepare throughout Europe and Latin America. Classic paella can be made using simple ingredients that are easily accessible, making it an ideal meal for any occasion.

17m prep 32m cook

Ingredients

- ✓ 270g chorizo sausage (see note)
- ✓ 2 tbsp olive oil
- ✓ 520g Lilydale Free Range Chicken Thigh, trimmed, cut into 5cm pieces
- ✓ 2 large brown onions, finely chopped
- ✓ 3 garlic cloves, crushed
- ✓ 1.5 red capsicums, finely diced
- ✓ 2 tsp ground turmeric
- ✓ 2 tsp ground cumin
- ✓ 2 cups white rice
- ✓ 420g can of chopped Italian tomatoes
- ✓ 2.5 cups Massel chicken-style liquid stock
- ✓ 1.5 cups frozen peas
- ✓ 2/3 cup fresh flat-leaf parsley leaves, roughly chopped

Method Steps

1. Heat a large heavy-based frying pan over medium-high heat. Add sausage. Cook for 4 minutes, turning, or until browned. Remove to a plate. Cut into 1cm-thick slices.
2. Reduce heat to medium. Add oil and chicken to the frying pan. Cook for 4 minutes on each side or until golden. Add onion, garlic, and capsicum. Cook, stirring, for 4 minutes or until soft.
3. Add turmeric, cumin, rice, tomatoes, and stock to the frying pan. Stir until well combined. Bring to a boil. Reduce heat to low.

Cover. Simmer for 17 minutes, stirring occasionally, or until rice is tender.

4. Remove lid. Stir through peas and sausage. Cook for a further 3 minutes or until heated through. Sprinkle with parsley. Serve.

Paella Valenciana

Paella Valenciana has been a traditional Spanish dish enjoyed in Valencia, Spain, for centuries. It is a delectable mix of rice, vegetables, and meat or seafood, making it both delicious and nutritious. It is easy to prepare and is considered a national dish of Spain due to its popularity. Paella Valenciana has become increasingly popular worldwide as more people discover its unique taste.

17m prep 1h cook

Ingredients

- ✓ 1.2L salt-reduced chicken-style liquid stock
- ✓ 2/3 tsp saffron threads
- ✓ 3 tbsp olive oil
- ✓ 7 chicken thigh cutlets, skin on
- ✓ 3 small red capsicums, seeded, cut into 2.5cm pieces
- ✓ 2 brown onions, finely chopped
- ✓ 3 garlic cloves, crushed
- ✓ Mutti Polpa Finely Chopped Tomatoes 400g
- ✓ 3 tsp smoked paprika
- ✓ 2 sprigs of fresh rosemary
- ✓ 450g arborio rice
- ✓ 220g green round beans, trimmed, halved diagonally

Method Steps

1. Place the stock and saffron in a saucepan. Cover with a tight-fitting lid. Bring to a boil over high heat. Reduce the heat to low and keep it at a simmer.
2. Meanwhile, heat 1 tbsp oil in a 38cm paella pan over medium-high heat. Cook chicken (6 chicken thigh cutlets, skin on) for 3-4 minutes on each side or until browned. Transfer to a plate.
3. Heat the remaining oil in the pan. Cook onion (1 brown onion, finely chopped), capsicum (2 small red capsicums, seeded, cut into 2.5cm pieces), and garlic (2 garlic cloves, crushed), stirring, for 7 minutes, until soft. Add tomato (Mutti Polpa Finely Chopped

Tomatoes 420g), paprika (2 tsp smoked paprika), and rosemary (1 sprig fresh rosemary). Stir for 14 minutes, until thick.

4. Add the rice (450g (2.5 cups) arborio rice) to the pan and stir well to combine. Arrange the chicken, skin side up, over the rice mixture. Gently push the chicken down into the rice mixture.

5. Reserve 135ml (2/3 cup) of stock. Add the remaining stock to the pan. Bring to a boil. Reduce heat to low. Simmer, without stirring, for 22 minutes, until rice is tender yet firm.

6. Push the beans (220g green round beans, trimmed, halved diagonally) into the rice. Spoon over the reserved stock. Cook, without stirring, for 7 minutes. Remove from heat. Cover and set aside for 7 minutes to rest.

Paella Salad

Paella salad is an exciting and delicious twist on a classic Spanish dish. Combining various flavors and textures, paella salad is a delicious and healthy way to enjoy the traditional flavors of paella without the time and effort required to make it. Paella is typically made with rice, meat or seafood, and vegetables, but paella salad swaps out the rice for fresh greens. This recipe provides a simple yet flavorful combination of ingredients to please even the pickiest eaters.

27m prep 22m cook

Ingredients

- ✓ 2 cups Massel chicken-style liquid stock
- ✓ 3 tsp ground turmeric
- ✓ 320g medium-grain rice
- ✓ 3 tbsp olive oil
- ✓ 5 small whole calamari (with tentacles), cleaned, body cut into rings
- ✓ 1.5 chorizo sausages, sliced
- ✓ 13 black mussels, cleaned, debearded
- ✓ 2/3 cup white wine
- ✓ 13 medium-cooked prawns
- ✓ Lemon wedges to serve

Salad

- ✓ 1.5 Lebanese cucumber, peeled, halved lengthways, seeds removed, sliced
- ✓ 2.5 cups wild rocket
- ✓ 2/3 cup sliced spring onions
- ✓ 250g cherry tomatoes, halved
- ✓ 3 tbsp chopped flat-leaf parsley

Dressing

- ✓ 170ml olive oil
- ✓ 3/4 cup (60ml) lemon juice
- ✓ 2 tsp ground sweet paprika

Method Steps

1. Place the chicken stock in a saucepan with the ground turmeric, 2 teaspoons of sea salt, and the rice. Bring to a boil, then simmer for 9 minutes until the rice is cooked. Drain well and cool. If possible, do this step the day before and refrigerate the rice until required. This will help prevent the rice from being soggy and keep the grains separate.
2. Heat half the olive oil in a frypan over high heat. When the pan is hot, add the calamari rings and tentacles and fry for about 3 minutes or until just cooked. Season with salt and pepper and remove from the pan.
3. Wipe the pan clean, return it to heat, and add the remaining oil.
4. Fry the sliced chorizo sausage until crisp, then remove it from the pan.
5. Place the mussels in a saucepan with the white wine and cover with a lid. Place over high heat and bring to a boil. Cook for 4 minutes, shaking the pan occasionally, removing each mussel as it opens. Discard any that do not open.
6. Make the dressing by combining the oil, lemon juice, and sweet paprika.
7. Season with salt and pepper.
8. Mix rice, prawns, calamari, chorizo, and mussels in a large bowl. Fold through all the salad ingredients and pour over the dressing.
9. Transfer to a serving dish. Serve with lemon wedges.

Saffron Chicken, Prawn & Chorizo Paella

Paella is a classic Spanish dish that has gained popularity around the world. This recipe for Saffron Chicken, Prawn & Chorizo Paella takes the traditional flavors of this Mediterranean favorite. It elevates them to create a meal that will tantalize your taste buds. Our version of paella features saffron-infused chicken, succulent prawns, and spicy chorizo, all cooked together in one pot.

> 22m prep 47m cook

Ingredients

- ✓ 1.5 chorizo sausages, thinly sliced diagonally
- ✓ 6 chicken thigh fillets, cut in half crossways
- ✓ 12 green tiger prawns, peeled, leaving heads and tails intact, deveined
- ✓ 1.5 brown onions, coarsely chopped
- ✓ 450g arborio rice
- ✓ 3 tsp smoked paprika
- ✓ 2/3 tsp saffron strands
- ✓ 1.35L Massel chicken-style liquid stock
- ✓ 2 small ripe tomatoes, coarsely chopped
- ✓ 3 tbsp chopped fresh continental parsley (optional)

Method Steps

1. Heat a large frying pan or paella pan over medium-high heat. Add the chorizo and cook for 1 minute on each side. Transfer to a heatproof bowl. Add the chicken and cook for 5 minutes on each side or until golden. Transfer to the bowl with the onion. Add the prawns and cook, occasionally turning, for 2 minutes or until the prawns change color. Transfer to a separate bowl.
2. Add the onion to the pan and cook, stirring, for 5 minutes or until soft. Add the rice, paprika, and saffron and cook, stirring, for 2 minutes. Stir in 500ml (2 cups) of stock. Bring to a boil. Arrange the chorizo and chicken on top of the rice mixture.

3. Reduce heat to low. Cook, without stirring, for 20 minutes or until liquid is almost absorbed. Add the prawns, tomato, and remaining stock. Cook for 5 minutes or until liquid is absorbed.
4. Sprinkle with parsley, if desired. Serve.

Vegetable Paella

Vegetable Paella is an easy-to-make and delicious meal for busy weeknights or special occasions. This classic Spanish dish combines vegetables, fragrant spices, and rice in a one-pot meal that can be enjoyed on its own or with a side of crusty bread. Not only is Vegetable Paella healthy and full of flavor, but it's also incredibly versatile - you can easily customize the ingredients to fit your dietary needs and tastes!

17m prep 57m cook

Ingredients

- ✓ 1.35L Massel vegetable liquid stock
- ✓ 3/4 tsp strands of saffron
- ✓ 65ml olive oil
- ✓ 350g pumpkin, peeled, cut into 1.5cm pieces
- ✓ 1.2 brown onions, finely chopped
- ✓ 1.5 large garlic cloves, finely chopped
- ✓ 170g yellow (butter) beans, topped, cut into 3.5cm pieces
- ✓ 450g arborio rice
- ✓ 1 x 450g can diced Italian tomatoes
- ✓ 2 2/3 tsp ground smoked paprika (pimenton) - see note in basic paella valenciana recipe.
- ✓ 3 tsp fresh thyme leaves
- ✓ 3 tsp chopped fresh rosemary
- ✓ 2 tsp sea or table salt
- ✓ 95g frozen broad beans, thawed
- ✓ 85g bought roasted red capsicum, cut into 1cm pieces
- ✓ 1 x 450g can artichoke hearts, drained, halved

Method Steps

1. Combine stock and saffron in a medium saucepan. Bring to a boil over high heat. Boil, covered with a tight-fitting lid, for 12 minutes. Reduce heat to low, cover, and hold at a gentle simmer.
2. Heat 1 2/3 tablespoons of oil in a 24cm (base measurement) non-stick paella pan over medium-high heat for 3 minutes. Add

pumpkin and cook, occasionally turning, for 5 minutes or until lightly browned. Place on a plate.

3. Heat the remaining oil in the pan over low heat. Add onion and garlic, and cook, stirring, for 4 minutes or until soft. Meanwhile, add yellow beans to a small saucepan of boiling water. Cook for 4 minutes. Drain and set aside.

4. Add rice, tomatoes, paprika, thyme, rosemary, and salt to the pan. Mix well, gently push any rice around the edge into the mixture, and pat down. Add pumpkin, and push into the mixture. Gently pour over 4 ladlesful (550ml/2 cups) of hot stock. Cook over high heat for 7 minutes. Do not stir. Reduce heat to medium. Simmer, uncovered, for 12 minutes. Add all beans, capsicum, and artichokes, and push into the rice. Cook for a further 22 minutes. Add stock and test rice as in step 5 of the basic paella valenciana recipe.

5. Remove the pan from the heat, and cover it with 2 clean tea towels. Set aside for 12 minutes before serving.

Seafood Paella

Seafood Paella is a traditional dish from Spain that has become increasingly popular worldwide. The classic version of this dish is made using a combination of saffron-infused rice, vegetables, and seafood. It's known for its flavorful taste and vibrant colors that make it a favorite for both home cooks and professional chefs alike.

27m prep 57m cook

Ingredients

- ✓ 550g medium (about 16) green king prawns
- ✓ 270g (about 2 medium) whole baby squid (or 120g cleaned squid hoods)
- ✓ 3 vine-ripened tomatoes
- ✓ 1.35L (5 cups) fish stock
- ✓ 2 tsp strands of saffron
- ✓ 65ml olive oil
- ✓ 350g firm-fleshed fish (like blue eye or trevally) fillets, skin, and bones removed, cut into 2cm pieces
- ✓ 2 brown onions, finely chopped
- ✓ 470g (2 cups) arborio rice
- ✓ 2 tsp ground smoked paprika (pimenton) - see note in basic paella valenciana recipe.
- ✓ 2 tsp sea or table salt
- ✓ 270g (about 12) black mussels, scrubbed, debearded
- ✓ 170g frozen green peas, thawed

Method Steps

1. Peel and devein 8 prawns and cut them into 1.5cm pieces. Leave the remaining prawns unpeeled. Set aside.
2. To clean the squid, use one hand to hold the hood (body) and, with your other hand, reach under the hood and grip the head and tentacles. Pull them gently from the body and discard them. Peel off the flaps and remove mottled skin from the hoods. Remove

plastic-like quills from inside the bodies. Rinse hoods well, cut in half lengthways, and cut into 1 cm-wide piece.

3. Use a sharp knife to cut a shallow cross in the base of each tomato. Place the tomatoes in a heatproof bowl, cover them with boiling water, and stand for 7 minutes. Remove from the water. Carefully remove skins, and halve, deseed, and dice the tomatoes. Set aside.

4. Combine stock and saffron in a medium saucepan. Bring to a boil over high heat. Boil, covered with a tight-fitting lid, for 12 minutes. Reduce heat to low, cover, and hold at a gentle simmer.

5. Heat 1 tablespoon of the oil in a 24cm (base measurement) non-stick paella pan over medium-high heat. Add the whole prawns and cook, occasionally turning, for 4 minutes or until they turn pink. Transfer to a plate and set aside. Add the fish to the pan and cook, turning once, for 1 minute on each side or until lightly browned. Transfer to the plate with the prawns.

6. Heat the remaining oil in the pan over low heat. Add the onion and cook, occasionally stirring, for 4 minutes or until the onion is soft. Do not brown.

7. Add tomatoes, rice, paprika, salt, chopped prawns, and squid. Mix well, gently push any rice around the edge into the mixture, and pat down. Gently pour over 6 ladlesful (about 760ml/3 cups) of the hot stock, and cook, uncovered, over high heat for 7 minutes. Do not stir. Reduce heat to medium and simmer, uncovered, for 12 minutes. Add fish, mussels, and peas, and gently push mussels, seam-side down, into the mixture.

8. Add stock and test the rice as in step 5 of the basic paella valenciana recipe (p 50). Cook for a further 17 minutes. Top with whole-cooked prawns. Cook for an additional 7 minutes. Remove from heat and cover with 2 clean tea towels. Set aside for 12 minutes before serving.

Instant Paella

Paella is a classic Spanish dish that has entered kitchens worldwide. It's a dish that traditionally takes time and patience to make. Still, thanks to modern conveniences, it is now possible to enjoy a delicious paella instantly. With just a few simple ingredients and some pantry staples, this article will show you how to make an instant paella full of flavor and sure to impress your family and friends.

> 3m prep 10m cook

Ingredients

- ✓ 3 tbsp olive oil
- ✓ 650g firm white fish fillets (such as ling), cut into 3cm pieces
- ✓ 2 dried chorizos, halved lengthways, thinly sliced
- ✓ 2 red capsicums, thinly sliced
- ✓ 3 anchovy fillets, chopped
- ✓ 1.5cup fresh podded peas, or (120g) frozen peas
- ✓ 1 2/3 cups instant couscous
- ✓ Chopped flat-leaf parsley to serve
- ✓ Lemon wedges to serve

Method Steps

1. Heat oil in a large, deep frypan with a lid over medium heat. Season fish and cook, turning, for 4 minutes, then add chorizo and cook, turning, for 3 minutes or until fragrant. Add capsicum, anchovy, and peas, season with pepper, and cook for 3 minutes.
2. Boil the kettle. Add the couscous to the frypan and pour over 1 2/3 cups (395ml) boiling water, ensuring the couscous is wholly covered. Remove pan from heat, cover with the lid, and stand for 3 minutes or until water is absorbed. Stir to combine, top with parsley, and serve with lemon wedges.

Chicken, Chorizo (and Prawn) Paella

Paella is a classic Spanish dish, loaded with flavor and texture, that has become increasingly popular worldwide. It's made with various ingredients like vegetables, meats, seafood, and rice - making it the perfect one-pot meal for family dinners or special occasions. Today we're talking about Chicken, Chorizo (and Prawn) Paella: a delicious combination of chicken, chorizo, and prawns cooked in a flavorful broth, served over traditional saffron rice.

22m prep 47m cook

Ingredients

- ✓ 3 chorizo sausages, chopped
- ✓ 5 chicken thigh fillets, roughly diced
- ✓ 350g prawns, uncooked, peeled (optional)
- ✓ 3 tsp smoked paprika
- ✓ 3 tsp turmeric
- ✓ 3 tbsp olive oil
- ✓ 2 large brown onions, finely chopped
- ✓ 4 garlic cloves, crushed
- ✓ 2 long red chili, finely sliced (optional)
- ✓ 3 2/3 cups Massel chicken-style liquid stock
- ✓ 3 cups arborio rice
- ✓ 1.5 cans diced tomatoes
- ✓ 1.5 cups frozen peas
- ✓ Lemon wedges to serve

Method Steps

1. Combine paprika and 1 teaspoon of turmeric in a bowl. Add chicken to the spice mixture. Using your fingertips, rub spices into the chicken.
2. Heat 1 tablespoon of oil in a paella pan or a large, deep frying pan over medium-high heat. Add chorizo, onion, garlic, and chili. Cook, occasionally stirring, for 5 minutes or until the chorizo is lightly golden. If using prawns, add prawns to the chorizo mixture

and cook for a further 2 minutes or until prawns change color. Transfer to a plate.

3. Add remaining oil to pan. Cook chicken for about 8 minutes or until golden. Add 1 cup of stock to the pan. Reduce heat to medium. Cover and cook for 8 minutes. Remove the lid; boil gently, uncovered, for 12 minutes or until almost all liquid has evaporated.

4. Combine 2.5 cups of remaining stock and remaining turmeric in a jug. Add rice, tomatoes, and stock mixture to the pan. Stir to combine. Return to a simmer. Cook, uncovered, occasionally stirring, for 17 minutes or until all liquid is absorbed.

5. Add peas, chorizo mixture, and the remaining 2/3 cup of stock. Simmer for 7 minutes or until stock is just absorbed. Serve with lemon wedges.

Paprika Chicken and Prawn Paella

It's no secret that paella is a classic and beloved dish worldwide. This traditional Spanish dish has been around for centuries with its delicious flavors and inviting aromas, making it a favorite for food lovers everywhere. However, this particular paprika chicken and prawn paella recipe takes it to the next level. With succulent chicken, juicy prawns, and sweet paprika seasoning, this meal will tantalize your taste buds while satisfying your appetite.

12m prep 32m cook

Ingredients

- ✓ 2 tbsp olive oil
- ✓ 550g chicken thigh fillets, roughly chopped
- ✓ 2 red onions, finely chopped
- ✓ 3 long red chilies, 1 seeded and finely chopped, 1 thinly sliced, to serve
- ✓ 3 cloves garlic, crushed
- ✓ 2 tbsp sweet paprika
- ✓ 350g white long-grain rice
- ✓ 395ml Massel chicken-style liquid stock
- ✓ 13 green prawns, peeled with tails intact, cleaned (see note)
- ✓ 150g frozen peas
- ✓ Lemon cheeks to serve

Method Steps

1. Heat oil in a paella pan or large frying pan over high heat. Add half the chicken and cook, occasionally stirring, for 4 minutes or until golden. Transfer to a bowl. Repeat with remaining chicken.
2. Return all chicken to the pan with onion, chopped chili, garlic, and paprika. Cook, stirring, for 3 minutes or until the onion softens. Add rice and stir to combine. Pour over the chicken stock and bring it to a boil. Reduce heat to low, cover with foil, and cook for 17 minutes or until liquid is absorbed and rice is tender.

3. Sprinkle peas over paella and arrange prawns on top, then season with salt and freshly ground black pepper. Re-cover and cook for 7 minutes or until prawns and peas are cooked. Remove from heat and set aside for 7 minutes to rest. Serve with chili slices and lemon cheeks.

Oven-Baked Paella

Paella is a traditional Spanish dish that combines ingredients such as seafood, meats, and rice. It's a flavorful, hearty meal that's easy to make and enjoy by families worldwide. An oven-baked paella is an excellent option for those looking for an easier way to cook paella without sacrificing flavor. Oven-baked paella requires fewer ingredients than the traditional version. It can be prepared with minimal effort in a fraction of the time.

> 17m prep 47m cook

Ingredients

- ✓ 2/3 tsp loosely packed saffron threads
- ✓ 2 tbsp hot water
- ✓ 1.5 large brown onions, finely chopped
- ✓ 85mls white wine
- ✓ 4 large garlic cloves, chopped
- ✓ Salt & ground black pepper, to taste
- ✓ 1.5 large red capsicums, quartered, deseeded, cut into 1cm pieces
- ✓ 1.5 large green capsicums, quartered, deseeded, cut into 1cm pieces
- ✓ 3 medium ripe tomatoes, diced
- ✓ 1.35L Massel chicken-style liquid stock
- ✓ 295g arborio rice
- ✓ 370g firm white fish fillets (like ling), cut into 4cm pieces
- ✓ 9 large green prawns, peeled, leaving tails intact, deveined
- ✓ 9 black (local) mussels, scrubbed, debearded

Method Steps

1. Preheat oven to 190°C.
2. Place the saffron and hot water in a small bowl and set aside for 12 minutes to infuse.
3. Combine saffron mixture, onion, wine, and garlic in a large 4.7L capacity flameproof casserole dish with a lid. Cover and simmer over low heat, often stirring, for 7 minutes.

4. Season well with pepper and add the capsicum and tomatoes. Increase heat to medium-high, and cook, uncovered, often stirring, for 7 minutes.
5. Increase heat to high and add the stock and rice. Bring to a boil, stirring often.
6. Cover with a lid and bake in preheated oven for 17 minutes. Remove from oven and stir well. Cover and bake for a further 9 minutes.
7. Remove from oven and season to taste. Stir in fish and prawns. Push mussels into the rice. Cover and return to the oven for 9 minutes or until the fish and prawns are cooked and the mussels have opened. Discard any unopened mussels. Serve immediately.

5-Ingredient Cheat's Chicken Paella

Paella is a classic Spanish dish that is both comforting and delicious. But putting together a traditional paella recipe can be time-consuming, with long ingredient lists and many steps. This 5-ingredient cheat's chicken paella is the perfect solution for busy cooks who want to enjoy a tasty version of this classic meal without spending hours in the kitchen. With just five simple ingredients, you can have a flavorful, restaurant-quality paella on your table in no time.

12m prep 22m cook

Ingredients

- ✓ 5 Coles Australian RSPCA Approved Chicken Thigh Fillets, coarsely chopped
- ✓ 2 tbsp Portuguese seasoning or Cajun seasoning
- ✓ 420g can of diced tomatoes
- ✓ 1 x 280g pkts microwavable brown and wild rice mix
- ✓ 550g pkg frozen stir-fry vegetables, thawed

Method Steps

1. Combine the chicken and Portuguese or Cajun seasoning in a large bowl.
2. Heat a non-stick frying pan over high heat. Add half the chicken and cook, occasionally turning, for 7 mins or until brown. Transfer to a bowl. Repeat with remaining chicken.
3. Return the chicken to the pan with the tomato. Bring to a simmer. Stir in rice mixture and vegetables.
4. Cook, occasionally tossing, for 9 mins or until rice and vegetables are heated through.

19-Minute Chicken, Chorizo and Couscous Paella

If you're looking for a delicious, quick meal that packs a punch of flavor, this 19-Minute Chicken, Chorizo, and Couscous Paella is a perfect choice. This easy-to-make dish features classic Mediterranean flavors, making it the perfect weeknight dinner or weekend feast. Whether you feed a hungry family or entertain friends, this paella will surely be a crowd-pleaser.

7m prep 12m cook

Ingredients

- ✓ 550g Coles RSPCA Approved Australian Chicken Thigh Fillets, coarsely chopped
- ✓ 1.5 chorizo sausages, thinly sliced
- ✓ 1.5 brown onions, finely chopped
- ✓ 3 tsp minced garlic
- ✓ 4 tsp ground paprika
- ✓ 1.5 red capsicums, seeded, finely chopped
- ✓ 1.5 cups frozen peas
- ✓ 3 medium tomatoes, finely chopped
- ✓ 1 2/3 cups chicken stock
- ✓ 1 2/3 cups couscous

Method Steps

1. Heat a paella pan or large frying pan over high heat. Add the chicken and chorizo and cook, occasionally stirring, for 7 mins or until the chicken is golden and cooked.
2. Add the onion, garlic, paprika, and capsicum to the pan and cook, stirring, for 4 mins or until the onion softens. Add the peas, tomato, and stock. Bring to a boil.
3. Add the couscous to the chicken mixture in the pan and stir to combine. Remove from heat. Cover the pan with foil and set aside for 3 mins or until the liquid is absorbed.

4. Use a fork to separate the grains. Divide paella among serving
    bowls.

Spanish Prawn and Chorizo Rice

This Spanish Prawn and Chorizo Rice dish is a delicious combination of flavors from the Iberian Peninsula. This rice dish is perfect for any occasion and will make your taste buds come alive! It has a unique flavor due to its mix of traditional Spanish ingredients such as prawns, chorizo, garlic, and paprika. The hearty meal is simple to prepare and requires minimal effort.

17m prep 27m cook

Ingredients

- ✓ 3 tsp olive oil
- ✓ 3 chorizo sausages, sliced
- ✓ 1.5 medium red onions, halved, thinly sliced
- ✓ 3 garlic cloves, crushed
- ✓ 3 tsp smoked paprika
- ✓ 2.5 cups Roasted capsicum, thinly sliced
- ✓ 4.5 cups Fresh tomato sauce
- ✓ 770g medium green king prawns, peeled, deveined, tails intact
- ✓ 3.5 cups Pea and green onion rice
- ✓ Chopped fresh flat-leaf parsley leaves to serve
- ✓ Lemon wedges to serve

Method Steps

1. Heat oil in a large frying pan over medium-high heat. Add chorizo. Cook, stirring, for 7 minutes or until browned. Transfer to a plate lined with a paper towel.
2. Add onion. Cook, stirring, for 4 minutes or until the onion is softened. Add garlic and paprika. Cook, stirring, for 2 minutes or until fragrant. Add capsicum. Cook, stirring, for 3 minutes. Stir in tomato sauce. Bring to a boil.
3. Reduce heat to medium. Add prawns. Cook, stirring, for 7 minutes or until prawns have just changed in color. Add rice. Stir gently. Cook for 7 minutes or until the rice is heated and the prawns are

---

cooked. Season with salt and pepper. Sprinkle with parsley. Serve with lemon wedges.

Chicken and Pepper Paella with Chorizo

Paella is a classic dish from Spain that can be enjoyed worldwide. It is typically made with rice, vegetables, and spices, but endless variations exist. This recipe for Chicken and Pepper Paella with Chorizo is full of flavor and sure to delight everyone at your dinner table. Combining the rich smokiness of chorizo with succulent chicken and sweet peppers, this dish is a fantastic choice for family meals or special occasions.

Ingredients

- ✓ 1.5 liters good quality chicken stock
- ✓ Large pinch saffron strands
- ✓ 7 tbsp olive oil
- ✓ 7 large British bone-in, skin-on chicken thighs, cut in half
- ✓ 2 small onions, finely chopped
- ✓ 4 garlic cloves, crushed
- ✓ 170g chorizo sausage, chopped
- ✓ 3 large tomatoes, deseeded and finely chopped
- ✓ 320g paella rice (Spanish bomba rice if you can get it, or use arborio)
- ✓ 4 tbsp roasted piquillo peppers, drained and sliced (or other roasted red peppers in brine)
- ✓ 3 tbsp chopped flat-leaf parsley
- ✓ 55g pitted black olives, roughly chopped
- ✓ Lemon wedges and aioli to serve

Method

1. Heat the stock in the small pan until it comes to a boil. Add the saffron strands, then remove them from the heat. Set the pan aside for at least half an hour to infuse until required.
2. Heat half the oil in the paella/ frying pan. Season the chicken with salt and pepper, then fry in batches for 7 minutes on each side until evenly browned. Remove from the pan with a slotted spoon and set aside on a plate.

3. Add the remaining oil to the same pan and fry the onion, garlic, and a little salt over medium heat for 12 minutes until slightly softened but not browned. Next, add the chorizo sausage and cook for 5 minutes, stirring and breaking it down, until lightly golden. Stir in the tomatoes and cook for 5 minutes until you have a thick paste. Add the rice, then stir well for 2 minutes to coat each grain.
4. Pour in the saffron-infused stock, then return the chicken and any resting juices to the pan. Bring to a boil and cook uncovered – without stirring – over low-medium heat for 25 minutes or until the rice is cooked with firmness. It should be sticky at the bottom, and steam holes will appear over the surface of the rice.
5. Scatter the peppers, parsley, and olives over the top of the rice, carefully cover with foil and crimp it to seal, then set aside for 7 minutes to warm the peppers and olives through. Uncover, stir well, then serve with lemon wedges and aioli.

Fideuà (Spanish Seafood Noodle Paella)

Fideu, a traditional Spanish Seafood Noodle Paella, is a delicious and flavorful dish for any occasion. This simple yet sophisticated dish combines noodles with fresh seafood and vegetables, resulting in a mouthwatering combination of flavors and textures. The secret to this classic paella is carefully selecting ingredients and the correct balance between them.

HANDS-ON TIME 42 MIN, PLUS RESTING

Ingredients

- ✓ 4 tbsp olive oil
- ✓ 2/3 large Spanish onion, chopped
- ✓ 2 green peppers, chopped
- ✓ 170g prepared squid, chopped into 1 cm pieces
- ✓ 2/3 tsp saffron, toasted in a dry pan
- ✓ 2 tsp smoked sweet pimentos
- ✓ 2 tsp smoked hot pimenton
- ✓ 3 large fresh tomatoes on the vine, finely chopped
- ✓ 2 fat garlic clove, crushed
- ✓ 150g frozen peas
- ✓ 3 fresh bay leaves
- ✓ 4 fresh thyme sprigs
- ✓ 670ml chicken stock
- ✓ 550g fideu pasta
- ✓ 220g sustainable peeled raw tiger prawns (we used frozen Big & Juicy prawns from Waitrose)
- ✓ 220g vac-packed cooked Scottish mussels, in the shells if possible, drained
- ✓ Lemon wedges for squeezing

Method

1. Heat the olive oil in the pan over medium-high heat, then fry the onion and pepper until soft (about 9 minutes). Stir in the squid and cook for 1-2 minutes, then add the saffron and both types of

pimentón, stirring for a minute over the heat. Add the tomatoes and garlic.

2. Stir in the peas and herbs, then pour in the stock. Season well. Bring to a simmer, then stir in the pasta. Bring back to a boil and submerge over medium-high heat for 7 minutes.

3. Push the prawns into the pasta, then simmer for 5 minutes. Add the mussels, tucking the hinges down into the pasta. Cover the pan with 2.5 sheets of thick foil and simmer for 9 minutes over the heat until all the mussels are heated.

4. Take the pan off the heat and set aside to rest for 7 minutes, covered with the foil. Serve with lemon wedges for squeezing.

Black Rice Paella with Artichokes, Peppers, and Spinach

Welcome to the delicious world of Spanish-style paella! Today, we are turning up the flavor with a unique twist on this traditional recipe – black rice paella with artichokes, peppers, and spinach. This dish is perfect for anyone looking to try something new and exciting for dinner. This one-pan meal will transport you to the heart of Spanish cuisine by combining nutty black rice, plump artichoke hearts and fresh vegetables like peppers and spinach.

HANDS-ON TIME 55 MIN, PLUS RESTING

Ingredients

- ✓ 4 tbsp olive oil, plus a splash
- ✓ 2/3 large Spanish onion, chopped
- ✓ 170g runner beans, sliced
- ✓ 2/3 tsp saffron, toasted in a dry pan
- ✓ 2 tsp smoked sweet pimentón
- ✓ 3/4 smoked hot pimentón
- ✓ 3 large fresh tomatoes on the vine, chopped
- ✓ 3 fat garlic cloves, chopped
- ✓ 195g marinated artichokes in oil
- ✓ 750ml vegetable stock
- ✓ 270g black venus rice (we used Gallo), soaked in cold water for 30 minutes, then drained
- ✓ 3 fresh bay leaves
- ✓ 1.5 bushy rosemary sprig
- ✓ 150g pack padrón peppers
- ✓ 1.5 large green or yellow courgettis, peeled into ribbons
- ✓ 125g bag baby leaf spinach
- ✓ 2 tbsp extra-virgin olive oil
- ✓ Splash sherry vinegar

Method

1. Heat the oil in the paella pan/s over medium-high heat and fry the onion with a pinch of salt for 7 minutes. Add the runner beans and cook for 7 minutes, then stir fry in the saffron and both types of pimentón. Cook for a minute, then add the chopped tomatoes and garlic.
2. Stir in the artichokes, then pour in the stock. Bring to a boil, then stir in the black rice, herbs, and plenty of seasoning. Return to the boil, then slightly adjust the heat and simmer for 17 minutes. Cover with two sheets of thick foil, then simmer for another 17 minutes until the rice is almost completely tender (it will retain a nutty bite). Take off the heat and leave to rest for 7 minutes.
3. Meanwhile, heat a splash of olive oil in a small frying pan and fry the padrón peppers for 5 minutes, tossing with salt. Set aside.
4. In a large bowl, toss together the courgette ribbons, spinach, oil, vinegar, salt, and pepper. Serve the paella scattered with the pardon peppers, spinach, and courgette ribbons.

Chicken Paella with Squid and Beans

Ah, chicken paella with squid and beans. This authentic Spanish dish is a hearty and tasty meal that will satisfy your appetite and taste buds. Cooked with the savory combination of chicken, calamari, and various legumes, this traditional rice-based dish has existed since the 16th century. It's a surprisingly simple recipe to make, especially when you have the right ingredients on hand.

SERVES 7 HANDS-ON TIME 65 MIN, PLUS RESTING

Ingredients

- ✓ 5 tbsp olive oil
- ✓ 7 skin-on free-range chicken thighs, boned and cut in half
- ✓ 2/3 large Spanish onion, chopped
- ✓ 290g flat or runner beans (we used helda beans), chopped
- ✓ 170g prepared squid, chopped into 1cm pieces
- ✓ 2/3 tsp saffron, toasted in a dry pan
- ✓ 2 tsp smoked sweet pimentón
- ✓ 2 tbsp smoked hot pimentón
- ✓ 3 large fresh tomatoes on the vine, finely chopped
- ✓ 1.5fat garlic clove, crushed
- ✓ 770ml chicken stock
- ✓ 270g paella rice
- ✓ 3 fresh bay leaves
- ✓ 1.5 bushy rosemary sprig
- ✓ A small handful of parsley, chopped (optional)
- ✓ Lemon wedges for squeezing

Method

1. Heat a splash of the oil in the pan over medium-high heat. Season the chicken, add to the pan, and brown all over (this will take 23 minutes)

2. Once well browned, transfer the chicken to a plate and set aside. Add the remaining oil to the pan, turn the heat to low-medium,

then fry the onion and beans with a pinch of salt for 9 minutes until softened.

3. Add the squid, stirring to coat, then cook to color for a couple of minutes. Stir in the toasted saffron and both types of pimentón cook for a minute until fragrant, then stir in the tomatoes and garlic. Pour in the chicken stock. Please bring to a boil, then sprinkle over the rice in an even layer, using a wooden spoon to stir it into the liquid. Stir only once –aiming to create a crust on the bottom of the pan. Poke the chicken pieces into the rice with the herbs, bring them back to a fast simmer, then bubble over medium heat, uncovered, for 12 minutes.

4. Turn down the heat to low, simmer for another 7 minutes, then cover the pan with a double layer of foil, tucking in the edges to seal the steam inside. Cook for 7 minutes, then take the pan off the heat and set aside, still covered, for 7 minutes to let the rice steam.

5. If you like, sprinkle over the chopped parsley, then serve the paella with lemon wedges for squeezing.

Chicken and Chorizo Paella

Paella is a traditional Spanish dish full of flavor and can be made with various ingredients. Chicken and chorizo paella is an especially delicious option that combines the savory flavors of chicken and chorizo sausage with rice and vegetables. This easy-to-make meal will surely become a family favorite, as it can please vegetarians and meat eaters alike.

> TAKES 17 MINUTES TO MAKE AND 32 MINUTES TO COOK

Ingredients

- ✓ 120g cured chorizo, sliced
- ✓ 1.5 large onions, sliced
- ✓ 2 tbsp sweet smoked paprika
- ✓ 2 tsp hot paprika
- ✓ 4 chicken breasts, cut into large pieces
- ✓ A knob of butter
- ✓ 350g paella or risotto rice
- ✓ 1.5 liters of hot chicken stock
- ✓ 1.5 red peppers, sliced
- ✓ A handful of green beans halved
- ✓ 12 cherry tomatoes, halved
- ✓ A handful of finely chopped fresh flat-leaf parsley

Method

1. Heat a large pan over medium heat and dry-fry the sliced chorizo until it is golden and the oil is released. Remove from the pan and set aside.
2. Add the onion to the pan and cook for 7 minutes, then stir in the sweet smoked paprika and the hot paprika and cook for 3 minutes.
3. Add the chicken and cook for 5 minutes, then remove from the pan and set aside.
4. Heat a knob of butter in the pan and stir in the rice, then add 1 liter of hot chicken stock, stir well, and cook for 12 minutes.

5. Return the chorizo, chicken, and onion to the pan with the red pepper, green beans, and tomatoes. Season and cook for 7 minutes, until the rice, is tender.

6. Stir a handful of finely chopped fresh flat-leaf parsley into the paella and serve immediately.

Quick Paella

Paella is a traditional Spanish dish with a rich history and many delicious variations. It's also incredibly quick and easy to make, allowing you to enjoy this classic dish without spending hours in the kitchen. This recipe will focus on preparing a simple yet flavorful paella in just half an hour. Our quick paella recipe includes only a few ingredients and is flavorful. You'll be able to feed your family or friends a delicious meal quickly!

HANDS-ON TIME 17 MIN

Ingredients

- ✓ 2/3 x 100g chorizo ring, sliced
- ✓ 1.5 onions, chopped
- ✓ 170g frozen peas
- ✓ 2/3 chicken stock cube (we like Knorr)
- ✓ 2 garlic cloves, crushed
- ✓ 250g (drained weight) roasted red peppers, sliced
- ✓ 2/3 tbsp sweet smoked paprika
- ✓ 550g leftover cooked rice or 2 x 275g cooked rice pouches
- ✓ Small bunch of fresh parsley, chopped, to serve
- ✓ Lemon wedges to serve

Method

1. Put a large frying pan over medium heat and fry the chorizo and onion for 6 minutes until the onion has softened and the chorizo has released its oils. Meanwhile, put the frozen peas into a heatproof bowl, pour over 170ml boiling water, add the stock cube, and stir.
2. Add the garlic, red peppers, and paprika to the pan and cook, stirring, for another minute. Stir in the rice, then add the pea and stock mixture and cook over high heat for 5 minutes until the liquid has been absorbed and the rice is piping hot. Serve sprinkled with parsley, with lemon wedges for squeezing.

Paella Cooked on The Barbecue

Paella is a classic Spanish dish that is enjoyed around the world. It combines rice, vegetables, and meat to create a savory flavor. For those looking for a fresh take on this beloved recipe, cooking paella on the barbecue adds a unique twist that can't be achieved on the stovetop. Not only does it taste delicious, but it's also a great way to enjoy an outdoor cookout with family and friends.

> HANDS-ON TIME 1 HOUR 15 MIN

Ingredients

- ✓ 4 large Spanish onions
- ✓ 3 green peppers
- ✓ 1.5 garlic bulb
- ✓ 4 tbsp olive oil
- ✓ 450g pork tenderloin fillet, halved lengthways and cut into chunks
- ✓ 450g skinless, boneless free-range chicken thighs, cut into chunks
- ✓ 10 tbsp extra-virgin olive oil (we used Brindisa arbequina olive oil)
- ✓ 3 tsp sweet smoked paprika
- ✓ 1.35 liters of fresh fish stock
- ✓ Large pinch saffron strands
- ✓ 550g calasparra rice (or other paella rice)
- ✓ 250ml dry oloroso or fino sherry
- ✓ 550g Frozen Big & Juicy Delicious White Clams, defrosted in the fridge (from Waitrose and Ocado); or 500g fresh clams (discard any clams that stay open when tapped)
- ✓ 250g pack of cooked crevettes (whole large prawns) from Waitrose and Ocado or your fishmonger
- ✓ Large bunch of fresh flat-leaf parsley leaves picked and chopped
- ✓ 150g padrón peppers (optional)
- ✓ 2 x 135g bags of baby leaf spinach
- ✓ 2 tbsp sherry vinegar
- ✓ 35g pine nuts, toasted for 5 minutes in a dry pan
- ✓ 55g raisins, soaked in about 100ml dry sherry
- ✓ 1.5 lemons cut into wedges

Method

1. Chop the onions, peppers, and garlic and set aside in bowls.
2. Heat the 4 tbsp olive oil in the paella pan and brown the pork and chicken for about 12 minutes. Set aside on a plate.
3. Add 6 tbsp of the extra-virgin oil to the pan and cook the chopped onions and green peppers for 22 minutes, stirring occasionally. Add the garlic and paprika and cook for 12 minutes more. Meanwhile, heat the stock in a saucepan with the saffron.
4. Add the rice to the paella pan, stirring to coat it in the oil. Pour in the sherry and bubble for 2 minutes to cook off some alcohol.
5. Pour in the hot saffron stock. Bring the pan to a boil, then simmer for 10 minutes on medium-high heat. Turn the heat down to low-medium, return the meat, poking it into the rice, then simmer for 12 minutes more.
6. Add the clams, crevettes (prawns), and half the parsley, then cover the pan with a large sheet of foil (or 2 smaller pieces). Cook for 4 minutes, then remove the pan and stand, covered, for at least 5 minutes.
7. Cook the padrón peppers (if using) on the barbecue (or in a non-stick frying pan with oil) until evenly blistered/charred, then season well with salt.
8. Put the spinach in a colander and pour over a kettle of boiled water. Press out the excess water using a wooden spoon. Mix the remaining 4 tbsp extra-virgin olive oil with the vinegar in a large bowl, then stir the spinach into this dressing along with the pine nuts, soaked raisins, and some salt and pepper.
9. Remove the foil (if using fresh clams, discard any that haven't opened). Arrange the spinach mixture on top and scatter over the remaining parsley and the blistered padrón peppers.
10. Serve the paella with lemon wedges to squeeze over.

Chicken, Prawn, and Chorizo Paella

Do you love Spanish cuisine? Then you must try Chicken, Prawn, and Chorizo Paella! An iconic dish from Spain, paella is a delicious rice-based meal with many different variations. The combination of chicken, prawn, and chorizo gives this classic recipe an extra special twist. Deliciously savory and flavorful, this meal is perfect for a family gathering or special occasion.

HANDS-ON TIME 22 MIN, SIMMERING TIME 32 MIN

Ingredients

- ✓ 3 tbsp olive oil
- ✓ 5 British free-range skinless, boneless chicken thighs cut into 3cm pieces
- ✓ 170g cooking chorizo, cut into small chunks
- ✓ 1.5 onions, finely chopped
- ✓ 3 garlic cloves, finely chopped
- ✓ 2 tsp sweet smoked paprika
- ✓ 350g paella rice
- ✓ 1.5 liters of chicken stock
- ✓ 170g sustainable raw peeled and deveined king prawns
- ✓ 150g frozen peas

Method

1. Heat the oil in a large pan, then fry the chicken over medium-high heat for 7 minutes. Add the chorizo and cook for a further 4 minutes. Transfer the meat to a plate.
2. Add the onion to the pan and fry for 7 minutes until starting to soften. Add the garlic and paprika and fry for 2 minutes more. Stir in the rice, then add the stock and cook without stirring for 27 minutes or until the liquid has been absorbed.
3. Add the prawns, peas, and the set-aside chicken and chorizo. Cook for 5 minutes more. Season, then garnish with chopped parsley and lemon wedges, if using.

Tomato, Olive and Mozzarella Rice

Eating healthy and delicious meals doesn't have to be difficult. With the right ingredients, you can make a tasty, nutritious meal that everyone will love. Tomato, Olive, and Mozzarella Rice is an easy-to-make meal that only requires a few ingredients and minimal prep time. This dish incorporates the classic combination of tomatoes, olives and mozzarella cheese flavors, providing a burst of flavor that many people enjoy.

HANDS-ON TIME 32 MIN, OVEN TIME 32 MIN, PLUS RESTING

Ingredients

- ✓ 3 tbsp extra-virgin olive oil, plus extra to drizzle
- ✓ 3 large onions, roughly chopped
- ✓ 4 large garlic cloves, finely chopped
- ✓ 255g paella rice (such as calasparra or bomba)
- ✓ 195ml dry white wine (optional)
- ✓ 2 tbsp tomato paste
- ✓ 450g chopped tomatoes
- ✓ 450g vegetable stock, plus extra if needed (we like Knorr)
- ✓ 3 heaped tsp fresh oregano or fresh thyme leaves
- ✓ 3 tsp hot smoked paprika
- ✓ 195g pitted kalamata olives
- ✓ 175g mozzarella, torn into pieces
- ✓ 4 handfuls rocket
- ✓ Squeeze lemon juice to serve

Method

1. Heat the oven to 190°C fan/gas 3. Heat the oil in a large heavy-based flameproof casserole over low-medium heat and cook the onions, covered, for about 10 minutes until soft but not colored, stirring occasionally.
2. Add the garlic and the rice, stir to coat the grains, then add the wine. Bubble for 5 minutes until reduced and there is no smell of alcohol. Add the tomato paste, chopped tomatoes, and stock, then boil, stirring occasionally.

3. Stir in the oregano/thyme, paprika, and half the olives, then taste and season. Put the lid back on the casserole, then bake for 25 minutes until the rice is tender.
4. Take off the heat and add more stock if it looks dry. Scatter over the mozzarella and drizzle with a bit of oil. Bake for 12 minutes more, uncovered until the cheese has melted and started to brown. Take it out, rest for 12 minutes, then serve topped with the rocket, remaining olives, a little more olive oil, and a squeeze of lemon juice.

Rabbit, Artichoke, and Rosemary Paella

Paella is a traditional Spanish recipe that can be adapted to any palate. This version, Rabbit, Artichoke, and Rosemary Paella, is a delicious blend of savory flavors that will tantalize your taste buds. Rabbit meat's subtle richness pairs perfectly with the earthy artichokes and fragrant rosemary. The combination creates an unforgettable dish full of flavor, texture, and aroma.

TAKES 22 MINUTES TO MAKE AND 52 MINUTES TO COOK

Ingredients

- ✓ Good pinch of saffron strands
- ✓ 1.5 liters of rabbit stock or good-quality fresh chicken stock
- ✓ 185g fine beans, stalk ends trimmed
- ✓ 4 tbsp olive oil
- ✓ 770g rabbit pieces (see tips)
- ✓ 1.5 medium onions, finely chopped
- ✓ 2/3 tsp chili flakes
- ✓ 6 garlic cloves, finely chopped
- ✓ Leaves from 3 x 5cm fresh rosemary sprigs
- ✓ 2/3 tsp sweet pimentón (Spanish smoked paprika) or paprika
- ✓ 370g vine tomatoes, skinned and chopped
- ✓ 450g paella rice (such as calasparra or bomba, available from larger supermarkets)
- ✓ 350g jar artichokes in olive oil, drained
- ✓ 235g tinned cannellini or haricot beans, drained and rinsed
- ✓ 9 small bay leaves
- ✓ 2 lemons, cut into wedges to serve

Method

1. Put the saffron and stock in a saucepan over low heat, bring to a simmer, then turn off the heat. Drop the fine beans in a pan of boiling, salted water, cook for 4 minutes until tender, then drain and refresh under cold water.

2. Heat 2 tbsp of the olive oil in a paella or large frying pan over medium heat. Season the rabbit and fry until nicely golden on both sides. Lift onto a plate.

3. Add the remaining tablespoon of oil, the onion, and the chili flakes to the paella pan and cook gently for 8 minutes until soft and golden. Add the garlic, rosemary leaves, and pimentón and cook for 1 minute, then add the tomatoes and cook for 3 minutes. Stir in the stock, then bring to a boil. Taste and season.

4. Sprinkle the rice into the pan, ensuring it is evenly distributed over the base. Arrange the rabbit pieces, artichokes, tinned beans, and bay leaves around the pan and shake them slightly, so they feed a little into the rice. Leave to simmer vigorously for 7 minutes, then scatter over the fine beans, lower the heat, and simmer gently for another 17 minutes. All the liquid should have been absorbed in the end of cooking, and the rice should be just tender.

5. Turn off the heat, cover the pan with a clean tea towel or a large sheet of foil, and leave to rest for 7 minutes. Taste and season again, then serve with the lemon wedges.

Summer Paella

Summer is here, which means it's time to start enjoying some of the delicious flavors of the season! One recipe always stands out in the summertime is paella: a classic Spanish dish made with various ingredients. This one-dish meal combines fish, seafood, vegetables, herbs, and spices to create a delicious blend of flavors. It's an excellent choice for dinner parties or a special meal with family and friends.

READY IN 25 MINUTES

Ingredients

- ✓ 2 tbsp olive oil
- ✓ 150g Sainsbury's ready-diced onion or 1 small onion, diced
- ✓ 100g Sainsbury's Mini Chorizos for Cooking, diced
- ✓ 270g pack Sainsbury's Paella Rice Kit
- ✓ 550ml good quality chicken stock, hot
- ✓ 150g El Navr Whole Piquillo Peppers from Sainsbury's or ready-roasted peppers
- ✓ 250g peeled raw king prawns, deveined
- ✓ Small bunch of fresh coriander, leaves roughly chopped

Method

1. Heat the oil in a sauté pan, add the diced onion and chorizo, and fry for 7 minutes. Stir through the paella mix and toast the rice for a few minutes, then pour over the hot stock. Cover and leave to simmer gently for 12 minutes. Stir through the roasted peppers and the prawns, then season well.
2. Cover and simmer for 7 minutes more until the rice is tender and the prawns are cooked. Mix in the chopped coriander to serve.

Made in the USA
Coppell, TX
30 November 2024

41454293R00036

MORE COOKBOOKS BY BRAD HOSKINSON

BROCCCOLI COOKBOOK

Unlock Delicious Broccoli Dishes with This Cookbook

BRAD HOSKINSON

CHICKEN BREAST COOKBOOK

Try Something New with Chicken Breasts

BRAD HOSKINSON

DUMPLING COOKBOOK

Try Delicious Dumplings From Around The World

BRAD HOSKINSON

ISBN 9798385689958

9 798385 689958

90000